111 Laws and Proverbs I Wish I Knew Earlier in Life.

111 LAWS AND PROVERBS I WISH I KNEW EARLIER IN LIFE.

Author: Samuel K. Anderson.
SamuelAnderson777.com

Books by Samuel K. Anderson

1. God's Audacity: The Logic of God's Existence.
2. Whispers from My Mother.
3. Human's Audacity: The Leadership in Everyone.
4. The Kind Prince and Princess (Children's Book edition)
5. Ascend to Your Higher Self
6. Energetic Vibrating Frequency
7. NINALEM: The Dawn of a New Era
8. Biblical Psychosis and Psychosomatics
9. Dear Afrikans, Can You Hear Me From 500 Years Ago or 500 Years From Today!!!
10. 111 Laws and Proverbs I Wish I Knew Earlier in Life.

Author: Samuel K. Anderson.
SamuelAnderson777.com

111 Laws and Proverbs I Wish I Knew Earlier in Life.

By

Samuel K. Anderson

Royal Publication

New Jersey, U.S.A

RoyalPublication777.net

Author: Samuel K. Anderson.
SamuelAnderson777.com

111 Laws and Proverbs I Wish I Knew Earlier in Life.

Copyright © 2020 Samuel K. Anderson.

All rights reserved. No part of this book may be reproduced or used in any manner without written permission of the copyright owner except for the use of quotations in a book review.

ISBN-13: 978-1-7340066-7-4 Paperback

Royal Publication

royalpublication@aol.com

Website: royalpublication.net

Author: Samuel K. Anderson.
SamuelAnderson777.com

111 Laws and Proverbs I Wish I Knew Earlier in Life.

This book is fervently dedicated to my children: Serenity, Samuel 2ⁿᵈ and Samuel 3ʳᵈ a.k.a Nana Datu.

Author: Samuel K. Anderson.
SamuelAnderson777.com

111 Laws and Proverbs I Wish I Knew Earlier in Life.

INTRODUCTION

111 Laws and Proverbs I Wish I Knew Earlier in Life is about the psychological and philosophical proverbs, self helps and attraction laws that position you to be your best self in every endeavor. The thoughts that roam through your mind have the power to become real life manifestations. These laws and proverbs are facts of every day life and science. Everything under the sun results from the acceptance and manifestation of good or evil, positive or negative energies or forces that gravitate manifestations. Practice these Laws of positive attraction, proverbs and wise inspirations that bring growth and success.

111 Laws and Proverbs I Wish I Knew Earlier in Life.

#1

Our own wickedness

becomes

our own punishment.

111 Laws and Proverbs I Wish I Knew Earlier in Life.

#2

Technology is a different form of spirituality. Science is another form of spirituality. Everything that manifests in the material world already exists in the spiritual realm. There are different forms of spiritual manifestations that transform essence (good or evil) from the spiritual world into this material realm. Everything seen and unseen, living or dead is related to the many forms of spirituality.

#3

We are all immortal though not in the flesh yet in the spirit we are as immortal as the image of *The Creator.*

Death can only hold the flesh for a moment passage of its last breathes as the spirit exits the flesh to its immortal life in eternity; just like vapor exits a hot surface.

#4

People Healing Intentionally Love Independent Peace Propelled In Newly Esteemed Self by Gradually Harnessing All New Awareness.

#5

A true leader must lead without fear or favor yet willing to adapt to the ever-changing times in order to stay current on issues and to develop tangible strategies capable of producing realistic results.

#6

In eating from the tree of knowledge; we rather became spiritually ignorant and physically docile than intellectually knowledgeable. In that, death, sickness, old age, and all kinds of troubles are upon us. We have traded living in eternity on earth with the Creator's presence to just a distant life in a jiffy full of troubles.

#7

God's audacity propels human's audacity. Human's audacity responds to God's audacity. The propensity of human's audacity manifestations is dependent on the propensity of *"God-like"* attributes sustained and awakened within us.

#8

Purposefully purporting your purpose is purpose pretentiously proclaimed which propels into oblivion.

111 Laws and Proverbs I Wish I Knew Earlier in Life.

#9

Everything in existence to the conscious mind of human beings is a small portion of everything in its existence in the grand scheme of nonexistence and spirituality.

#10

Knowledge doesn't hurt anyone, it just releases us from intellectual imprisonment.

Knowledge is the first step to gaining wisdom. Knowledge can be falsified; some are rare and true.

Test every knowledge to find which constitutes the truth.

Seek knowledge daily. It's necessary to pursue knowledge if you truly want to be free.

#11

Everybody was created/born to be extra-ordinary. Some of us choose the hard route to be ordinary by starving our mind, body and spirit.

To get back to your original extra-ordinary self. You will need to be aware of the starvation in order to find the right nutrients to feed your mind, body and spirit.

#12

In my candid logic of reasoning, common sense and wisdom is far greater than knowledge; in that, knowledge can be manipulated and controlled but wisdom always reign supreme.

#13

The difference between you and I

is that you think you know me

but I know very well that I know myself.

Hence, the reason why I move the way I move.

I talk the way I talk.

I walk the way I walk.

I speak the way I speak.

Thinking you know me is where you fell off;

because I really don't care about what you think.

Knowing myself is key to my being.

111 Laws and Proverbs I Wish I Knew Earlier in Life.

#14

At this very moment, what's going on in your mind? Are you analyzing all the problems in your life with your family, friends, career, and the universe to the point that you are literally lost in your own existence?

Right this moment, this very micro-second that just passed; what have you been thinking of? Are you feeling like you hit rock bottom and all hope is lost? Are you in a panic mode? Feeling anxious and overwhelm at the same time? The good news is that, you and I control everything that goes through our mind. You and I can pick and choose what we want to analyze through our mind. You and I have the audacity as human beings to request, require, demand and prophesy into our *now* and our *future*. So, cheer up and make the best outcome of your current situation come true.

111 Laws and Proverbs I Wish I Knew Earlier in Life.

#15

When you fall,

make sure; you do not go into hiding.

Do not be ashamed of your failures.

Do not run away from the issues that

caused your fall

rather, face those issues head-on.

Be accountable for what you did right

and wrong.

Learn from both sides.

Prepare yourself for a better comeback.

111 Laws and Proverbs I Wish I Knew Earlier in Life.

#16

Having the rapacious propensity for agglomeration with acquisitive conglomeration is a clear indication of a failed bonafide psychological emancipation in a pathological world of illusive dogmatism.

#17

Don't hesitate to wake the genius in you.

Feed it.

Exercise it.

Pay attention to it.

Above all, give that genius in you a

chance

to do what it was meant to do and see

what happens.

111 Laws and Proverbs I Wish I Knew Earlier in Life.

#18

In this universe, we have codes that are made specifically for each person. Inside the codes are your individualistic extraordinary significance.

There are specific keys for all the codes. Whenever you are ready, just use your keys to unlock your ordained codes to open the doors to your reason of being. Remember, no one can access your codes; if you fail to use these codes before your time on earth expires then you will be buried with these codes.

Use them while you can breathe in and out.

#19

We discredit many opportunities than granting opportunities to all the opportunities that come to us in our lifetime.

111 Laws and Proverbs I Wish I Knew Earlier in Life.

#20

Be succinct in your ways

to strategically think through things

in order to succinctly communicate

through actions with integrity,

accountability

and probity.

#21

Strategically strategizing the strategies are key to striking home most of the strategic strategies strategized.

#22

A woman of grace,

elegance and wisdom

is a rare kind of distinction

calmly waiting within every woman

ready to be woken.

111 Laws and Proverbs I Wish I Knew Earlier in Life.

#23

Every human being can literally maximize anything they want or desire to maximize.

Some of us fail because we tend to maximize the wrong things instead of the right ones.

Maximization is at the front door of everyone. Just open your door to your world of unlimited maximization.

111 Laws and Proverbs I Wish I Knew Earlier in Life.

#24

If you have the power to say anything to yourself and the power to become anything you choose to become then why do you decide to choose less and say some of the meanest things about yourself?

Why do you choose:

Bondage over Freedom?

Worrier over Warrior?

Fear over Confidence?

Temporary over Eternal?

#25

The darker you are the stronger the energetic field of attraction. The source of the god-like energy is the Melanin.

You are mocked.

You are discriminated against.

You are tortured. You are wrongfully accused.

You are hated for no reason.

Your natural hair, looks, energy and being are always envied.

Because you are everything, they wish they could be. The source of your melanin is the *Melanated Creator* of all things known and

111 Laws and Proverbs I Wish I Knew Earlier in Life.

unknown to every creation. You are rare. You are

The Creator's heartbeat. You are a part of the air

The Creator breathes.

They all feed off of your energy.

Regain your conscious power.

Regain your spiritual power.

Regain your physical power.

Regain your God-ordained melanin.

You already have it. The code is already infused in you.

You are a god directly from God.

You are powerful from the Omnipotent.

You are present from the Omnipresent.

You are conscientious from the Omniscient.

#26

The truth is like a rare treasure hidden from the masses as lies are given out as everyday dosage.

111 Laws and Proverbs I Wish I Knew Earlier in Life.

#27

It was a quiet morning, you could hear a feather drop

on the floor.

I stare in lost escape as the hand of the clock tick tocks away;

revealing to me the immeasurable opportunities in every second

of its movement.

Was that time, space and life crunching

their precious moments at my pleasure?

Was that a signal of exhibition whispering

all the astounding things yet to happen?

Was that time, space and life igniting my

much anticipated purpose in this physical

realm? Shivers of euphoria transmitting

through every inch of my neurons.

I got up from my dazed position to strike

at all the endless possibilities that this

intimate moment gifted to me.

111 Laws and Proverbs I Wish I Knew Earlier in Life.

#28

We are all here on a mission. Every single one of you including all living things.

We all have platforms to deliver our message and services regardless of how small or big our platforms may be.

Our mission begins with a heartbeat right when the electronic energy successfully strikes the diploid cell, known as zygote.

Some missions are prematurely terminated by the mother ship housing the messenger(s). The mission and the message

111 Laws and Proverbs I Wish I Knew Earlier in Life.

are delivered consciously or unconsciously from the homeless, the rich, the middle class, the poor, the brave, the timid, the deceiver, the peace keeper, the warmonger, the spiritual ones, the soil mixing organisms and the list goes on.

When it's all said and done, we are terminated from this physical dimension to our true self; spiritual beings.

111 Laws and Proverbs I Wish I Knew Earlier in Life.

#29

If you believe in the existence of any spiritual entity or the devil however criticize others who believe in God;
then you are basically not on the path of philosophy, wisdom, or spirituality.

Who has seen God?

Who has seen the devil?

Who has seen "fear"?

Who has seen "love"?

None of these entities/energies are seen
yet, we all feel "loved", "afraid", as well as believe in "love" and expressions of "fear".

If one is imaginary, then; are all not imaginary?

Your acceptance of one over the other doesn't make any of them nonexistent.

Author: Samuel K. Anderson.
SamuelAnderson777.com

111 Laws and Proverbs I Wish I Knew Earlier in Life.

#30

Water is very essential

to life's sustainability

but the same water

can easily kill someone;

however, that doesn't reduce

the important quality of water.

#31

Be true to your core.

The tune to the culture doesn't change.

It is who you are, your roots.

Why are you confused?

Why are you begging?

Don't you know you are the chosen?

The magnet of your strength is in unity.

So, why do you hate thy brother?

Why do you reject your own?

Now, you see why you are powerless?

Come back to your senses.

Stand for what you believe.

Do not ever be afraid of another man.

You must stop wandering.

Turn on the music to the tune of your consciousness.

Arise, unite immediately and fight together as one.

Now, is the time. Unite, unite, unite!

#32

Do not be intimidated by another person's wealth, greatness and influence. You have equally important and effective treasures of greatness in you. Tap into it and be your own kind of person of valor.

#33

When you try too hard,

usually nothing comes out of it.

The outcome is dependent on what I call,

the intent of manifestation.

111 Laws and Proverbs I Wish I Knew Earlier in Life.

#34

Time doesn't run out.

Do not fall for the pressure of time.

Time is an illusion.

There are not twelve months in a year.

Some civilizations have ten months; others have thirteen.

Do not fall for the pressure rather push for your passion.

What makes you free, that's your light and that's how you are supposed to move in this space and moment.

#35

Whenever you catch yourself

making too much noise;

run a quick self-assessment to

see how full or how empty you are

then make a wise decision based on

the outcome of the self-introspection.

#36

Integrity is the tool

needed

for versatility that reflects

one's longevity.

#37

Daily welcoming fears in your life

to cripple you from pursuing your

aspirations

is just like purposefully welcoming

daily nightmares in your dreams.

#38

The birth of every child

is the birth of a new generation.

It remains our responsibility

to properly educate every new generation

that we are blessed with to be better

than previous generations for a better

posterity.

#39

I used to struggle to accept

the phrase, " there's time for everything"

until I learned that

patience, knowledge, hope and wisdom

are necessary to understand the concept

of time and my role in it all.

#40

My heart has many thoughts

and many thoughts come to my mind

but at the end of the day; it's my mind

that determines what thoughts stays

and what thoughts are thrown out

through the windows of my heart.

#41

What is happening

are things that are supposed

to happen to pave way

for the good things that are meant

to happen to happen.

111 Laws and Proverbs I Wish I Knew Earlier in Life.

#42

You are not for everyone.

Your dreams are not for everyone.

Your energy is not for everyone.

Your goals, gifts and talents are not for everyone.

You were not created or born for everyone.

Your mission on earth is not for everyone.

Your physical and spiritual consciousness are not for everyone.

So do not live a life that yearns for everyone's approval.

You will be accountable after this life,

it doesn't matter whether you accept it,

believe it or deny it.

Live your life because you are responsible

of your life and will be held accountable for it.

Author: Samuel K. Anderson.
SamuelAnderson777.com

#43

At some point in this life,

we free ourselves from ourselves.

Don't hold yourself captive till the very end.

#44

At your discretion as much as you are in control of your mind and spirit; you have the power to rebuke as many times as possible anything that your gut tells you that it doesn't belong to your life's purpose.

#45

Do you just love

the thought of me,

the presence of me,

the existence of me,

the beauty of me with or without makeup,

the strengths I exhibit,

or

the fullness of me with all my imperfections yet to be

known to you.

Because,

I am more than what you think of me.

I am a spiritual being,

I am a conscious soul,

within this flesh that drew your attention.

111 Laws and Proverbs I Wish I Knew Earlier in Life.

#46

Fear will easily destroy your world before it destroys your life. This world will fail because we have allowed fear to be a reason to destroy each other regardless of our differences and indifferences.

#47

The shortfall of a youth is to think that everything last forever. It feels majestic in youthful days but make sure to seize those majestic moments to secure a formidable future of wisdom, grace, success and awareness.

111 Laws and Proverbs I Wish I Knew Earlier in Life.

#48

If you fail to read,

research, study and

dig deeper for answers

then you widely open yourself

to be swayed by those who

seize the moments to read,

research, study and dig deeper.

#49

In the midst of all

the chaos, bickering

and backbiting in the world;

be madly committed

to enjoying your own vibe in life.

#50

Every relationship deserves honesty

no matter how small or big the situation

may be.

Be true with your feelings to

communicate

them with your partner;

especially, the most difficult or

complicated ones.

111 Laws and Proverbs I Wish I Knew Earlier in Life.

#51

Every day, you have one hundred percent option to choose either life or death. Some choices illuminate lifelong blessings while others trigger lifelong curses. Every single day is a terrific opportunity to exercise such freedom of life or death.

111 Laws and Proverbs I Wish I Knew Earlier in Life.

#52

There are different entities living

within the man in the mirror.

Dreamers live in *Dreamland*.

Action takers live in *Actionland*.

Doers live in *DoerLand*.

Fear lives in *Fearland*.

Success lives in *Successland*.

Beasts live in *Beastland*.

Love lives in *Loveland*.

Wisdom lives in *Wisdomland*.

Determination lives in *Determinationland*.

All these entities can travel

through and live at various lands with

the sole permission by the man in the mirror.

#53

There are going to be times that you may make some mistakes as a leader, a teacher, a motivator or a legacy setter. When confronted by these mistakes, don't allow your ego of achievements deprive you from humbly acknowledging and learning from your mishaps. This could be one of the simplest yet toughest lessons of discipline to you.

#54

Fear or favor may only take you so far

in this life on planet earth

but your effort in putting in the work is

needed

to live a life free of fear and uncertainties.

#55

No human being can confidently claim to never have been angry. When you get angry just try your best to think about your favorite person or favorite place in your life; that's a workable trick for me.

111 Laws and Proverbs I Wish I Knew Earlier in Life.

#56

Go all in on taking risk.

Yes, all in as in one hundred percent.

Fail all out, flat out.

Win all out, clean and strong.

111 Laws and Proverbs I Wish I Knew Earlier in Life.

#57

One of the many secrets I have personally learned through life is to never settle no matter how undulatingly tortuous my circumstances may display. Rather to revolve to involve to evolve in revolutionary replicability rendered via re-setting, re-focusing, re-evaluating, refreshing, re-strategizing, re-educating and re-charging.

#58

Show me all those

that are failing in life

and I will show you

what they are doing right.

111 Laws and Proverbs I Wish I Knew Earlier in Life.

#59

The road to success hurts.

It can hurt your ego.

It will hurt your pride.

It hurts your confidence.

Sometimes, you can even feel

the pain of depression and rage.

That's what makes the destination

worthwhile. Once you have experienced

the adrenaline and mastered maneuverability;

you begin to be so addicted to success that you are

always willing to go through the journey all over

again.

#60

Sometimes we may get distracted while pursuing the goal/purpose. It is human nature for that to happen, do not beat yourself up. Discipline your mind to stay determined to the journey.

Stay focus through the realms of perseverance. For it is only then would you be able to accomplish your goals/purpose in life.

111 Laws and Proverbs I Wish I Knew Earlier in Life.

#61

There's something called life. No living person can cheat it. It will handle you with no mercy if you keep on screwing up. It has its own moments of punishments and rewards. Happy is the one who gains its blessings.

Learn to be good to it.

Be true to it.

Appreciate it.

Enjoy it.

Use it as a service to others.

Learn from it.

Grow with and within it.

This is something that all living things must go through with no exception.

Author: Samuel K. Anderson.
SamuelAnderson777.com

#62

It is better to live

a short life full of virtues

than a long life full

of wickedness and destruction.

#63

If you can buy all the fanciest clothes, cars, houses and other material things yet struggle to buy books upon books upon books then you may be misplacing some of your priorities.

111 Laws and Proverbs I Wish I Knew Earlier in Life.

#64

One of the most difficult lessons to learn in life is the art of humility, as it requires you to lower your ego and exposes your vulnerabilities; yet, it's one of the utmost rewarding attributes needed to excel at almost everything in life.

#65

Creativities of the creative are geared by creative ambitions and thoughts of the creator.

#66

Heal and continue to heal so high that you are able to heal yourself from a higher altitude and to heal others when the need arises.

#67

Snap out of your illusions.

Snap out of your sleep.

Snap out of your self-inflicted mental slavery. Regardless of who deceived or forced you to take the pill of illusion that caused your tranquilized sleep; you have the power to decide to set yourself free.

#68

One of the easiest ways

to live life is to laugh at things

you do not understand

but that's also one of the most

foolish ways to live your life.

#69

Don't doubt yourself.

Let them flow.

The unlimited passion,

drive, actions, dreams, plans,

service, burning desire, fulfillment,

and imaginations.

Let them all flow through you;

absorb them all.

#70

Fools are simply arrogant. Arrogance breeds ignorance which leads to a shameful fall.

111 Laws and Proverbs I Wish I Knew Earlier in Life.

#71

Infinity is not infinity

if you do not think of it

as infinity.

111 Laws and Proverbs I Wish I Knew Earlier in Life.

#72

Happiness, good health, peace of mind, pure love, heart of joy and a beautiful soul are all pure energies that we decide to either embrace or reject. If you look into your life and you feel empty or missing any of these life energies; just make a conscious decision to attract, embrace and hold on to as many of these positive life-filled energies as possible. It's your choice, your personal decision to make.

Author: Samuel K. Anderson.
SamuelAnderson777.com

#73

We all see the world differently

and it mostly depends on the way

we were brought up

and what we were exposed to;

never allow that to cripple you

from becoming the best version of

yourself

no matter your upbringing.

#74

Show me what you desire to accomplish.

List the steps you have already taken.

None? Well, get started.

Few but haven't worked?

Well, try harder;

Use different approach.

#75

He who is able to control his emotions can withstand almost any adversity by thinking and planning strategically through application of the philosophy of common sense.

111 Laws and Proverbs I Wish I Knew Earlier in Life.

#76

The moon and back

is just the beginning

of my love for you.

What can be!

What will be and

What is yet to come

Are all just a wonder

in my infinite plethora

of love for you.

Come my dear,

Take my hand and

Let's soar into the dimension

of infinite love.

#77

Confidence is a key ingredient to success. Your confidence will be tested by opposing forces. The strength and level of your confidence would be vital to how far you go in life.

Can you keep on going when no one believes in you? Would you give up when even your closest friends, family and sometimes your partner doesn't side with the journey?

Your confidence can make or break you. Build your confidence up every day. If you believe in what you are doing, then no matter the objection; you ought to make sure to keep on pushing for your goal.

111 Laws and Proverbs I Wish I Knew Earlier in Life.

#78

One of the best freedoms in this life

is psychological freedom.

The ability to take control of

your conscious self from all the viruses

in this world is definitely one

of the ultimate freedoms in life.

Author: Samuel K. Anderson.
SamuelAnderson777.com

#79

Good psychological

and physical health

are richer and worthwhile

than billions of gold.

#80

The thoughts of a person without the guidance of wisdom is corrupt and yield results planted in greed, selfishness and destruction.

#81

When you set the goal so high.

You are definitely going to be petrified and that's okay. You may even think about doing a 180 turn around to give it all up; that feeling is okay too.

However, under no circumstance should fossilization by petrification engulf your aspirations.

Keep the accelerator in place and keep driving forward.

#82

Look into the mirror.

Now, stare very hard

and deeply into your eyes.

Close your eyes for a second, open them.

What do you see?

Ask yourself, who am I?

Make sure your answer is exactly who

you need to be.

111 Laws and Proverbs I Wish I Knew Earlier in Life.

#83

We all have the ability.

The ability to use your ability

to attain your abilities is your

ability. The level of your ability

is set by your ability to recognize

your endless abilities.

Hence, the ability of your abilities

is your own ability.

#84

Do not focus on the feelings of the word; rather focus on the truths of the word.

#85

As the man of the household, your leadership is more important than the amount of money you make for the family. The wife and children see your exemplary leadership and through that, the pace and outcome of the family are set. A man is a man for a reason and a woman is a woman for a reason too. Do not lose focus of this important core instituted by *The Creator*.

111 Laws and Proverbs I Wish I Knew Earlier in Life.

#86

Our life on earth is as relatively short as food entering and exiting the alimentary canal. Why do you boast of things that you don't rightfully own? You came into this world naked and you will surely exit the same way. As a reminder, just take a look at yourself whenever you shower or bath. We all enter the shower or bath tab naked and exit out of it naked. This is another daily reminder to remain humble and fearful in reverence of The Most High God of your ancestors.

#87

Words can undress you

and it's not only sapiosexuals,

but the same words can address you

and dress you with a covering

of dignity and respect.

#88

A mind willing to explore

is a mind capable to be free.

#89

In this journey, make sure you surround yourself with those that support you and that include your haters.

Your haters are some of the most brutally honest supporters you need to have around you, not close to you.

Trust me, they are there to pump you up; they themselves don't even know about that yet.

#90

Admire great talents and gifts of others but never be jealous of them. Be inspired by them to aspire for your talents to be manifested.

111 Laws and Proverbs I Wish I Knew Earlier in Life.

#91

Within each one of us lies greater

and lesser selves of yourself.

Lesser people decided to choose

their lesser selves instead of their greater self.

Great people decided to choose

their greater selves instead of their lesser selves.

The work, discipline, mindset, accountability

and determination needed to become

either self is dependent upon which self

you decide to choose.

These choices are found within your

reason of being; your purpose in your

existence.

Author: Samuel K. Anderson.
SamuelAnderson777.com

111 Laws and Proverbs I Wish I Knew Earlier in Life.

#92

Show me who will pass on a certified assurance and I will show you a foolish person.

111 Laws and Proverbs I Wish I Knew Earlier in Life.

#93

Don't be afraid to face

your worse self

because

that's the best way to correct it.

#94

We sometimes fall.

We rise.

We stand tall.

We wiggle in low confidence

or we push through confidence

and all these things happen because of

words.

Words are powerful wavelengths of

immeasurable energy.

111 Laws and Proverbs I Wish I Knew Earlier in Life.

#95

It's a challenge to change a mind that has been heavily indoctrinated with hundreds of years of lies believing that he or she is not capable of leading, achieving massive successes and walking in greatness. It's a great challenge but it can definitely be done.

#96

One of the tests you will face is seeing the ones you love uninterested in seeking knowledge or wisdom and being destroyed in their complacency yet unbothered to even try to free themselves from their psychological deficiencies in most cases until it's too late.

#97

Be confident in your ways

and never be ashamed

or apologize for your confidence;

however, be diligent to admit when you

know that you are wrong.

111 Laws and Proverbs I Wish I Knew Earlier in Life.

#98

If tomorrow never comes,

then today never ends.

Tomorrow's plans are plans of hope,

belief and the faith of a better encounter

greater than today.

… # #99

Believe, believe, believe, believe!!!

For that's the fuel

to drive your actions

to its destination.

111 Laws and Proverbs I Wish I Knew Earlier in Life.

#100

To be discovered by the world

and the people in it, you need

to be discovered by yourself.

There is no grand discovery

without self-discovery.

111 Laws and Proverbs I Wish I Knew Earlier in Life.

#101

For tomorrow to be better

you ought to start today,

turn on your ignition;

regardless of your momentum.

#102

Edify yourself with the right things.

Take care of yourself daily.

Seek wisdom, knowledge, love and grace.

You have total control in what you absorb.

Make sure you are drinking from the fountain of purified consciousness, spirituality and balance.

Edification through sanctification is paramount to self-actualization in both physical and spiritual realm of your being.

111 Laws and Proverbs I Wish I Knew Earlier in Life.

#103

There is absolutely

no love without

self-love. You can

never change that phenomenon.

Author: Samuel K. Anderson.
SamuelAnderson777.com

111 Laws and Proverbs I Wish I Knew Earlier in Life.

#104

Everything in creation living and non-living move through time, space, waves and sounds.

The fact that you cannot detect its movement doesn't defy its performance of movement.

What's important is for you to identify your rhythm within all the three heavens and on planet earth.

That's only when you may come close to all the movements happening through time, space, waves and sounds.

Author: Samuel K. Anderson.
SamuelAnderson777.com

111 Laws and Proverbs I Wish I Knew Earlier in Life.

#105

To love yourself is to embrace discipline,

to embrace discipline is to be astute,

to be astute is to be diplomatic,

to be diplomatic is to be lighthearted,

to be lighthearted is to be amour propre.

#106

Remove every cataract that obstructs your flow of progress.

Break the chain that restrain your passion.

Invest heavily in your mind. The power to full liberation is strongly dependent on the muscle strengths of your mind.

#107

You cannot grow spiritually without growing physically and consciously.

111 Laws and Proverbs I Wish I Knew Earlier in Life.

#108

Be aware.

Be alert.

Be resolute.

Be informed.

Be knowledgeable.

Be persistent.

Be daring.

Be a fighter.

Be a believer.

Be resilient.

Be confident and persuasive.

Be brilliant.

Be a repetitive failure.

Be stubbornly determined to bounce back.

Be useful of grit.

Be fearless.

Be adventurous.

Be daring.

Do not be timid or intimidated regardless of your circumstance.

Author: Samuel K. Anderson.
SamuelAnderson777.com

#109

Take a moment to observe

your scars.

Each scar represents a moment,

or a situation in your life.

These scars represent a time

of transitional growth or bitter

lessons. Your scars should be your

motivation to create a better

situation for yourself at present to

the future. Cherish them, appreciate them

and embrace them because those scars

are part of your whole being.

111 Laws and Proverbs I Wish I Knew Earlier in Life.

Author: Samuel K. Anderson.
SamuelAnderson777.com

111 Laws and Proverbs I Wish I Knew Earlier in Life.

#110

Your strength and durability

are tested at every

phase of life that

requires perseverance.

111 Laws and Proverbs I Wish I Knew Earlier in Life.

#111

We have been deceived to chase things

that cost us an arm and leg

making us lifeless and heartless

while depriving ourselves from things

that are free and priceless like laughter,

happiness, joy, appreciation, good rest,

and self-love.

111 Laws and Proverbs I Wish I Knew Earlier in Life.

THE END

Author: Samuel K. Anderson.
SamuelAnderson777.com

111 Laws and Proverbs I Wish I Knew Earlier in Life.

PEACE

LOVE

UNITY!!!

Author: Samuel K. Anderson.
SamuelAnderson777.com

About The

AUTHOR:

Samuel K. Anderson (MBA, BSBA, University of The Incarnate Word) is a Ghanaian Nigerian American citizen and a member of the largest leadership honor society in the nation (United States of America) known as NSLS, The National Society of Leadership and Success. He has served as an astute leader, motivator, philanthropist, father, entrepreneur, mentor, wisdom seeker and educator. He is a vibrant CEO and founder of two companies. A motivational and life coach speaker.

He has impeccable hands-on experience in banking, real estate, bankruptcy, life insurance, compliance, risk Samuel K. Anderson management, estate, probate, foreclosure, and investments. He served in his early formal education years as the Regional Trustee for the Eastern Regional Students' Representative Council with the Council's aim to Emancipate Students through Dialogue and a Philosophy of Non-Violence, President of an NGO that aimed at educating the youths on drug abuse, Counselor and Director of Children's Ministry. He completed formal bible training education/Seminary School and also studied Theology at Central University College before transitioning to San Antonio College then transferred to University of The Incarnate Word to pursue bachelor's degree in Accounting and an MBA with concentration in Asset Management (Real Estate and Finance).

Author: Samuel K. Anderson.
SamuelAnderson777.com

111 Laws and Proverbs I Wish I Knew Earlier in Life.

www.ingramcontent.com/pod-product-compliance
Lightning Source LLC
Chambersburg PA
CBHW070953080526
44587CB00015B/2294